The Philosopher Cat

ALSO BY KWONG KUEN SHAN

The Cat and the Tao

www.kwongkuenshan.net

The Philosopher Cat

KWONG KUEN SHAN

WILLIAM HEINEMANN: LONDON

Published in the United Kingdom in 2004 by
William Heinemann

1 3 5 7 9 10 8 6 4 2

William Heinemann
The Random House Group Limited
20 Vauxhall Bridge Road, London, SW1V 2SA

Random House, Australia (Pty) Limited
20 Alfred Street, Milsons Point, Sydney,
New South Wales 2061, Australia

Random House New Zealand Limited
18 Poland Road, Glenfield, Auckland 10,
New Zealand

Random House (Pty) Limited
Endulini, 5a Jubilee Road, Parktown 2193,
South Africa

The Random House Group Limited Reg. No. 954009
www.randomhouse.co.uk

A CIP catalogue record for this book
is available from the British Library

Papers used by Random House are natural, recyclable products made from wood grown in sustainable forests. The manufacturing processes conform to the environmental regulations of the country of origin

Design & make-up by Roger Walker

Typeset in Monotype Joanna

Printed and bound in Singapore

ISBN 0434 01310 2

GRATEFUL THANKS TO

The cats in my life: Healey, Joseph and Rocco, Joseph's brother, who left home for good when he was two years old.

The cats I know: Angus, Homer, Nimble, Peppy, Samarui, Felix, Benson, Bijou, Saffron, Heidi, Monty, Rosie, Leo, Little cat, Joshua, Coco, Lily, Colin, Oscar and Maculous Mousens.

The many people who kindly let me paint their cats for this book.

My cat-loving friends, in particular Ingrid Pieters and Ruth Field, who share with me lots of cat anecdotes and laughter, not forgetting the support and tears shared in moments of need.

These cats and their people have taught me a lot. Knowing them has enriched my life.

Finally, my husband, Christopher, whose technical support in preparing this book for publication enables me to focus all my time and effort on the brush strokes and whose patience and skill in removing bodies, 'alive or dead', brought in by our cats, have saved me many heart attacks.

INTRODUCTION

Since the publication of *The Cat and the Tao* painting cats has become a very important part of my work.

My two cats Healey and Joseph have become my partners at work, they provide me with endless ideas and inspiration.

I watch them, observe them. They watch me, they take notice of me.

I used to fear cats, to avoid them at all costs. Joseph and Healey have socialised me into their unique world. I have learnt a few things about cats since my cat phobic days!

They come and go as they wish. Once they are outside I don't know where they go or what they are up to. They never report back, never share their secrets with me, but I have learnt to trust them. They do not obey, but they don't disobey either. They always come home and are always around.

I find their thundering purr, upturned tail, big round eyes and full whiskers charmingly and determinedly persuasive. I always give in to their demands.

I have observed that cats are their own men, with their own set of rules. They do not have possessions nor do they owe anyone anything. I find their body language a pleasure to watch. One minute they are sitting there, motionless, looking into space, meditating, or just dozing, a picture of serenity and elegance, next minute they are on high alert, sniffing, listening, stalking, pouncing and hunting. Whatever they do is played out in the most athletic and mesmerising style. I can watch them for hours.

Some people say cats have no facial expressions. I agree, but I watch their eyes. Cats' eyes say a million words, so round, clear and knowing, holding ancient mysteries and a hundred secrets which I will never get to know.

Cats mind their own business. They live for the moment, reacting to what is happening now and are totally oblivious of what may or may not happen. They don't have plans, ambitions, fantasies or imagined fears. I find some of these qualities admirable and refreshing. Watching them is like reading a fascinating new book I cannot put down. Except with this book the central characters are real and are living with me.

Once you are tuned into cats all your birthday and Christmas presents come with whiskers and paws. You meet people who like cats. You meet cats themselves, some funny, some serious, some timid, others fierce, never humble, but all beautiful in their own way.

I took advantage of my new-found inspiration and resource. I carried on painting cats.

Hundreds of sketches later I developed 40 paintings for *The Philosopher Cat*.

To complement these paintings I have selected and translated text from old Chinese classics, proverbs, Tang Dynasty poems and Zen teaching. The majority of the text is from ancient philosophers and teachers, mainly Confucius, Mencius, Lao Tse and Chong Tse.

The teachings of these masters were recorded, preserved, handed down through generations and have helped shape the behaviour and moral conduct of the Chinese for centuries. Their teaching is not doctrines or rules. They are templates for wisdom and truth on life and living. They point a way for those who wish to seek truth, harmony and peace in their everyday life. These templates are timeless with no racial, religious or geographical boundaries. They hold truth and relevance to anyone, anywhere at any time.

In preparing this book for publication I have spent many solitary hours rereading volumes of Chinese literature and philosophy. When I studied Classical Chinese in Hong Kong I had to memorise many selected sayings. My teacher said to me, 'one fine day, you may understand their wisdom!' My 'one fine day' came many years later when I was living and working abroad. Yesterday I studied them as a scholar. Today I read them as a grown-up with life's responsibilities and desires. I interpret the writing with new eyes!

The choice of texts in this book is based on personal taste and their interaction with my paintings. I have attempted to interpret and translate the quotes to the best of my understanding. I hope I have gone some way in preserving the wisdom and truth of the original writing.

I hope you enjoy the book and I hope you find some comforting thoughts in the evergreen wisdom of ancient China.

Kwong Kuen Shan,
2004
http://www.kwongkuenshan.net

1. THE CHINESE CALENDAR

Near the dawn of time, Buddha held an audience. He invited all creatures on earth to attend.

On the day only 12 individuals answered his summons. To show his generosity and to thank them for their courtesy, Buddha devoted a year to each of the twelve animals who came, in order of their arrival on the day. They were the rat, ox, tiger, rabbit, dragon, snake, horse, goat, monkey, rooster, dog and the pig. From this came the twelve zodiac signs of the Chinese calendar. Each animal is thus the symbol of the year that is named after it. Those born under a particular sign carry the characteristics and behaviour traits of that animal.

The cat did not answer the summons. It spent the day sleeping.

I have my own ways, I do not conform,
No one owns me, I lead my own leisurely life.

CHINESE COUPLET

Chinese characters: Cats are fun | Square seal: Kwong Kuen Shan | Oval seal: Heaven and earth

2. SIX KITTENS

The rat says: I am a charmer and a great conversationalist.
The ox says: I am reliable and dependable.
The tiger says: I dazzle people, I am a natural leader.
The rabbit says: I am kind and considerate. Luck is always
     on my side.
The dragon says: I am an independent soul. People admire me.
The snake says: I am simply irresistible.
The cat miaows.

When the majority dislike a person, it is important
     to find out why;
When the majority like a person, it is also important
     to find out why.

CONFUCIUS

Chinese characters: Ox, Rabbit, Snake, Rat, Tiger, Dragon
Square seal: Kwong Kuen Shan | *Oval seal: Follow your destiny* | *Small seal: Blessing*

3. FOUR KITTENS

The horse says: I am an optimist. People love my company.
The goat says: I am artistic. I love beautiful things.
The monkey says: I am decisive and courageous.
The rooster says: I am self-assured and honest, but leave me alone!
The cat purrs.

A man who does not look for deceit, lies or dishonesty from
his fellow men, but who knows them when he sees them, is
a wise man

CONFUCIUS

Chinese characters: Rooster, Monkey, Goat, Horse
Square seal: Kwong Kuen Shan | *Oval seal: Heaven and Earth* | *Small seal: The way*

4 . TWO KITTENS

The dog says: I am responsible and honest. I make a loyal friend.
The pig says: I am ambitious and hardworking. Oh, I am
    so successful!
The cat hisses.

Everything in the world exists for a reason
Do not compare yourself with other people
Do not undervalue yourself
Do not over estimate yourself.

ANON

Chinese characters: Dog, Pig | *Square seal: Kwong Kuen Shan* | *Oval seal: My painting*

犬貓

緹珊

5. THE RESIDENT

Achievement and fame are like morning dew
Wealth and honour are just floating clouds
Life is a dream we are all passing through
Home is where you find comfort and peace

CHINESE COUPLET

6. CHRYSANTHEMUM

Flowers bloom every year.
Youth, once it is gone, will never return.

CHINESE PROVERB

7. RAIN SHELTER

A breeze does not last the whole morning.
A shower does not go on for the whole day.
Natural occurrences do not last forever;
Nor does a man.

TAO TE CHING

8. THE THREE OF US

People can learn together but go different ways,
Go the same way but achieve different standing,
Stand together but have different aspirations and judgement.

CONFUCIUS

Chinese characters: Be as calm as still water and insight and understanding will come
Square seal: Kwong Kuen Shan | Oval seal: My painting | Round seal: Pre-determined fate

其靜如水 靈悟巧思

緣

娟珊

9. THE CHINESE FIGURINE

We used to meet in the Imperial court,
Where you sang many times before.
We both love the scenery on the south bank of the river.
Now the blossoms are falling fast,
And here we meet again!

THE MEETING, BY DU FU, TANG DYNASTY

Chinese characters:Who in this world does not know who you are!
Square seal: Kwong Kuen Shan | Small seal:The moon in water

天下谁人
不识君

娟珊

10. MY CHINESE SIDEBOARD

If destiny wants you two to meet,
You will come together although you come from a
    thousand miles apart.
If destiny does not want you to know each other,
You remain strangers even if you stand face to face.

CHINESE PROVERB

Chinese characters: Pre-determined fate | *Square seal: Kwong Kuen Shan* | *Oval seal: Heaven and Earth*

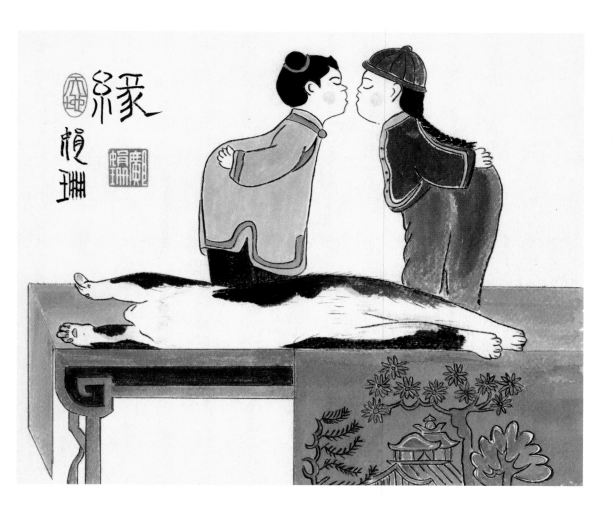

11. THE IMPERIAL GUARD

This night fine wine glowing in shimmering glasses,
I am drinking to the music of Pipa.
The bugle calls and I am summoned to the battle field.
If you find me lying drunk in action,
Do not laugh or sneer my friend,
How many warriors in the past returned safe and sound.

THE BATTLE FRONT BY WANG HAU, TANG DYNASTY

12. THAT OLD POT

I do not walk with someone who is prepared to fight a tiger with bare fists, nor with someone who would walk across a river to face death with no regrets.
I prefer the company of people who are cautious and plan their actions to achieve the desired results.

CONFUCIUS

13. TECHNOCAT

At work give 100 percent.
At play give 100 percent.
Do not dream of play while at work.
Do not think of work while playing.
This way you get the best out of both work and play.

ANON

14. ORCHIDS

The year is long, busy people make it short
The world is vast, narrow-minded people make it small
Nature is full of beautiful things
Worriers do not see them, miss their beauty and a whole lot more!

ANON

Seal: Kwong Kuen Shan

15. WHERE THE CHASE ENDS

The whole world praises me, I will not try harder
The whole world criticises me, I will not feel deflated.

CHONG TSE

Chinese characters: Above the crowd | *Square seal: Kwong Kuen Shan*
Small seal: Blessing | *Rectangular seal: The way*

16. SUMMER THOUGHTS

In solitude I have discussions with ancient sages and
    masters through my thousand books:
In leisure I stroll in my garden of trees and flowers to
    enjoy nature's company.

CHINESE COUPLETS

Seal: Kwong Kuen Shan

17. SUMMER DREAMS

One who understands the meaning of life does
    not pursue the meaningless:
One who understands the destiny does not pursue
    things which are beyond him.

CHONG TSE

18. COCO AND LILY

One who thinks himself foolish is not the most foolish;
One who thinks himself confused is not the most confused.
The truly confused never understands;
The truly foolish never acquires wisdom.

CHONG TSE

19. THE COLLECTOR

Fame and wealth do not stay forever,
They come at random and stay for a while.
Accept them when they come,
Release them when they go.

CHONG TSE

Square seal: Kuen Shan | *Long seal: The brush expresses my feeling*
Small square seal: Blessing | *Small long seal: The way*

20. THE MANDARIN CATS

When you arrive at a place, follow the tradition of the place, observe the customs of the people.

CHONG TSE

21. LEISURE

A person who does not pay attention, looks but does not
see, listens but does not hear, eats but tastes nothing.
The mind must focus the senses to make such a person
concentrate.

THE GREAT LEARNING

Chinese characters: Leisurely moments bring great enjoyment
Square seal: Kwong Kuen Shan | Oval seal: As my heart desires | Round seal: No regrets

閒情逸致

娟珊

22. AGEING GRACEFULLY

At 15 I made up my mind to study

At 30 I established myself

At 40 I developed clear vision

At 50 I understood the will of God

At 60 I heard and received the truth

At 70 I followed my heart without overstepping the boundary.

CONFUCIUS

23. XENA

The wise man finds pleasure in water:
Like flowing water he is active and moving forward ceaselessly.
The virtuous man finds pleasure in the mountains:
Like them he is solid and calm.
The wise man pursues joy and knowledge;
The virtuous man pursues tranquillity and long life.

CONFUCIUS

Square seal: Kwong Kuen Shan | Round seal: Insight

24. THE UNDERSTUDY

What the leader likes
His subordinates like even more.
It is like wind and grass:
When the wind blows, the grass bends

MENCIUS

25. INSTINCT

Retreat from the race when you have achieved your goal:
This is to follow nature's law.

LAU TSE

Square seal: Kwong Kuen Shan | *Oval seal: Heaven and Earth*

26. HERMAN'S CASTLE

Fish swim freely in the sea but do not notice the water,
Birds fly freely in the sky but are not aware of the space,
Men live freely in the world but tie themselves down
    with burdens and worries.
When you understand the true meaning of freedom
    you rise above all these to enjoy nature's way.

CHONG TSE

Seal: Kwong Kuen Shan | *Long seal:The brush expresses my feeling*

27. DESIRE

Do not rush to complete a task;
Do not be greedy over small gains.
Rush and you will not complete the task properly;
Greed over small gains will hinder great achievement.

CONFUCIUS

28. YOUNG ATHLETES

Stand on your toes and you cannot stand for long;
Jump to go forward and you will not go far.

LAU TSE

Square seal: Kwong Kuen Shan | *Round seal: Chi — the vital energy* | *Small seal: Blessing*

29. FOCUS

The eye is the most truthful part of the man's body,
The eye does not hide evil intentions:
If the heart is straightforward the eyes shine,
If the heart holds evil intentions the eyes dull and empty;
Listen to a man and watch his eyes,
You will see his real character.

MENCIUS

Top square seal: Kwong Kuen Shan | *Bottom square seal: Forever*
Round seal: Do not fight over gains and losses

30. LITTLE CAT

The breeze bestows freshness,
The moon bestows brightness.
When active I watch the river flow,
When thoughtful and in need of solitude I turn to the mountains.

CHINESE COUPLETS

Seal: Kwong Kuen Shan

31. POWER STRUGGLE

When interacting with a superior you can make three errors:
To speak when you are not supposed to, you are hasty;
To keep quiet when you should speak, you are hiding something;
To speak without first noting his facial expression, you are blind!

CONFUCIUS

Square seal: Kwong Kuen Shan | *Small seal: Blessing*

32. THE WARNING

Life and death are unavoidable cycles,
Like day and night they are natural rhythm;
When life comes, you cannot resist,
When life ends, you cannot stop it ending.

CHONG TSE

Square seal: Kwong Kuen Shan | *Small seal: Blessing*

33. BETHAN

I practise three principles which I hold close to my heart
One is to be kind, Two is to be frugal, Three is to be modest.
Being kind I have courage, Being frugal I can be generous,
Being modest I can lead.
These days people abandon kindness for mere bravado,
Abandon frugality for extravagance,
Abandon modesty for power and control,
All these bring disasters

TAO TE CHING

Square seal: Kwong Kuen Shan | *Oval seal: My painting* | *Small seal: The way*

34. LITTLE FRIENDS

Heaven and earth are fair in the treatment of all creatures:
When you hold a high position do not think you are a
    step above the rest of the world,
When you occupy an inferior position do not think you
    are a step below the rest of the world.

CHONG TSE

Chinese characters:We are friends the moment we meet | *Square seal on left: Forever*
Square seal on right: Kwong Kuen Shan | *Round seal: Do not fight over gains and losses*

一見如故

娟珊

35. THE SECRET

When two people get on everything they say to each other is
    sweet and positive
When they don't get on, every word is bitter and provocative

CHONG TSE

36. MY PERFECT CAMOUFLAGE

Do not argue with the world over gains and losses
Do not allow life's trivialities to determine your ups and downs

CHINESE COUPLETS

Square seal: Kwong Kuen Shan | *Long seal: The brush expresses my feeling*

37. I WALK ALONE

A brave warrior is not intimidating,
A great fighter is not easily provoked,
A winner is not vindictive,
A good superior is modest.
This is the virtue of non-competitiveness,
This is making the best of people,
This is matching the way of nature.

TAO TE CHING

38. MY ROSE GARDEN

Don't be blinded by temptation
Don't be deafened by outside interferences
Don't burden your heart and mind with worries
Guard your senses and spirit
They will guard your body and soul

CHONG TSE

Seal: Kwong Kuen Shan | *Round seal: Chi - the vital energy* | *Small round seal: Insight*

39. MEMORIES

In building a home, site matters
In thinking, depth matters
In dealing with people, kindness and generosity matter
In talking, honesty matters
In leading people, justice matters
At work ability matters
In decision making, good timing matters
If you do not compete with other people
Winning or losing does not matter

TAO TE CHING

Chinese characters: Forget me not | Square seal: Kwong Kuen Shan
Long seal: Descendant of the dragon | Round seal: Things pass by but they are never gone

EXPLANATORY NOTE ON SEALS

Seals you see on Chinese paintings are Chinese characters carved in jade, ivory, soapstone or wood. They are pressed into cinnabar paste and then pressed in a suitable position on the painting to reproduce the characters.

Chinese writing characters come in different forms of scripts some of which are thousands of years old. In this book I have presented a collection of seals using different types of scripts in different shapes and types of stones.

There are two main types of seals. One is the name seal which bears the name of the painter. The other is the 'mood' or 'leisure' seal which bears Chinese characters to reflect the feeling, mood, inspiration or philosophy of the painter.

My painting

Chi – the vital energy

Forever

Things pass by but they are never gone

Do not lose your temper

No regrets

Life is just a dream

Kwong Kuen Shan

Do not fight over gains and losses

The brush expresses my feeling

As my heart desires

Heaven and Earth

Pre-determined fate

Descendant of the dragon